# DISCLAIMERS:

One of Kim Porter's final wishes,
was for this Memoir/Diary to be made public...

Out of protection for certain parties,
and their potential criminal activity,
some celebrities, performers, and events,
have been represented with X's,
due to their highly explosive nature.
At some point in the future,
this information will be revealed to the public.

Regarding Kim's sudden death,
and the mysterious illnesses of Al B. Sure and Jamie Foxx,
evidence does exist,
that points to foul play and/or poisoning.

**God Bless Kim Porter,
and all of Sean Combs' victims,
both male and female.**

# TABLE OF CONTENTS:

# CHAPTER 1:
## INTRODUCTION

Soon after high school I started landing modeling jobs, I couldn't believe it. It was all happening so fast. I met my husband, father of my oldest child, and one of my oldest friends in life, Al B Sure. It was a whirlwind romance. I was only nineteen when we married, and no, it didn't work out. Al is still one of my best friends to this day. Our son Quincy is such a talented, and wonderful young man.

At that time, I had no idea my relationship with Al was going to introduce me to the man that I would spend the better part of my adult life with, a man whom I would love and cherish, but eventually, fear and hate.

I don't want to put the cart before the horse, but I will say, although I knew what was going on, I turned a blind eye many times. Here I have to tell this truth, unfortunately, because deep down I knew everything that was happening, but I lied to myself a lot.

He was so charming, a wolf in sheep's clothing. A devil, and I fell for it. This story must be told despite the fact it will hurt my children. I cannot hide it any longer.

Sean Combs must be stopped.

## CHAPTER 2:
## HUMBLE BEGINNINGS

I was born to loving parents Jake Porter, and Sarah L. Porter in the Peach State of Georgia. All through Columbus High School, where I graduated in 1988, I knew I was going to be famous. In the tenth grade one of my best friends, Tina said to me, "You won't make it here in Georgia". I knew if I really wanted to be famous, I would have to leave my hometown, and my home, Georgia. That conversation was so important as I look back now. It changed my life!

I met Al while I was working in the industry. He was so dope and charming, and I had such a crush on him. We were married before I knew it, and Quincy was on the way. But I was young, and it just felt like it wasn't going to last.

It was a little heated between us after we separated, but we got past that quickly. He is just a super dope guy, and an amazing father. Though we separated, we are forever bonded through Quincy. Thank you, Al, I will always love you.

When I met Sean, he was cool. I didn't think much of him at the time, he was just another guy at the label. Uptown was huge, and we were all living our best life. But Sean continued to lay on the charm, and before I knew it, we were dating. As a young single mom at one of the hottest companies in the world, life couldn't get any better. Then it did. My boyfriend was getting even bigger!

He and Clive would hang out a lot. But I didn't think anything of it. I mean that was his boss, and he was doing things bigger than most men dare to even dream. Then it happened. I mean, okay, I was a little bit of a freak. I really enjoyed myself with my partner, and toys are one thing, but I never imagined having a man I was dating, asking me to use a toy on him.

The first time, he said he just wanted to experiment, try something new. I was grossed out, but he kept begging. He said it would only be this one time, and he was just curious. I was only twenty at the time. I said what the hell. I hated it. He bled from it, and there was shit on it.

I left him alone after that.

CHAPTER 3:
SECOND CHANCES


Sean kept reaching out, and I kept ignoring his calls. Eventually, in a few weeks we ran into each other at an event. He came over and sat next to me. We were cordial. He flattered me by saying, "You look so amazing." I replied with a simple, "Thanks, Sean." I tried to get up to leave, but he pulled my arm, as I turned to him, he looked deep into my eyes and said, "Look, what happened between us was weird. But I really care about you. Can we…"
He paused, and I tried to use this as my attempt to escape. I pulled my hand back and said, "Sorry Sean, I have to go." "Please I think I'm falling in love with you. Can we talk?"
My breath was taken away. Did he say he loved me? It was so fast. I wasn't aware of this as his manipulation tactic, not yet. God I was so young, so naïve.
He continued, "Let's just have dinner." And I fell for it. Two days later we went out for drinks at a lounge in Lower Manhattan. The place was nice. Sean was really coming up, and pulling out all the stops to impress me. He pulled the chair out for me to sit. Back then, he was always a gentlemen. He smiled and said, "Look," as he sat across from me, "I hated it, and I never want to do it again. Give me another chance." Over coffee the next morning, I decided to give him another chance.

For the next year-and-a-half, things seemed pretty normal. It was fun. Things were going great, and we were living the dream that I dreamt about throughout my youth. Sean and Clive were working on Bad Boy, and he had his first couple of artists. He picked up Craig Mac, then some rapper from the West Coast called Notorious B1, to help Chris develop. He was collaborating with the biggest names in Hip-Hop to make it happen. Things could not be more amazing!

Then he asked me to do it again. It was insane. Sean said, "Baby, I can't stop thinking about it." "What the hell are you talking about?", I responded. Sean continued, "I just can't stop thinking about that night. It was amazing. Can you screw me one more time, Please?!" I became infuriated, "Why don't you go to Clive! He is the one screwing you, isn't he?" Then Sean hit me. This was the first time, but he slapped me hard. Before I could form words, he began to beg, "I'm... I'm sorry." Holding my cheek where he hit me, I turned and ran off. That should have been it. But I guess I am a glutton for punishment.

He sent flowers, and a bunch of expensive gifts. Then we bumped into each other at another industry event. He sat down next to me. This was Deja vu. Sean started, "Imagine running into you here.". "Get the fuck away from me!", I forced out. He became more serious as he said, "Look, baby I'm sorry.", but I just glared at him, "There is nothing you can ever say to me. Nothing." After an awkward silence, he finished, "You know I love you. I love your son. He's my son. I don't know how to fix this, but I'll do anything. I'm sorry." Shit, he can be so sweet. Here we go with the love thing. This time it's not 'falling in'.

He was great with Quincy, and to be honest, despite everything, I missed him. As he stood to walk away I remember hearing myself saying, "Call me later."

What the fuck is wrong with me?

## CHAPTER 4:
## FORGIVENESS

Sean arrived with flowers in hand, he wanted to see Quincy. He was so good with him, and Quincy ran over to hug him. I felt my heart melting. He asked Quincy. "How you doing, Tiger?" Quincy looked so innocent as he responded, "I'm good. I miss you." Sean's response sounded genuine, "I miss you, too." "We'll hang out tomorrow, okay?" "Okay." Sean gave him a little love tap on the butt, "It's bedtime." Quincy replied, "Okay, good night," as he turned to head toward his bedroom.

Here was the man I fell in love with, but what was I thinking? Shit, not only does he want butt plugs, he slapped the shit out of me. So, why am I still talking to him? They say that love is blind, but is it stupid, too?

As Quincy left, Sean looked at me and smiled, "Baby, let's go have some fun. The babysitter is on the way. I just want to show you a good time." I was so mad at myself for melting as I said, "Okay." We sat on the couch laughing and genuinely having a good time when the doorbell rang. The babysitter had arrived, and so we left. As we exited the house a big man climbed out of the limo and opened the door for us. He wore a sharp suit with a gun noticeably tucked under his arm. I thought to myself, 'He could have made it invisible, or did he want me to see it?'

Despite my reservations, Gene was a sweetheart. He was very courteous and polite, as he tipped his head and said, "Good evening, ma'am." Gene drew a smile out of me, as I responded, "Hello."

Gene and I would see each other a lot after this day.

## CHAPTER 5:
## SEAN KNEELS

The year passed and (thankfully) we didn't have many bad arguments, although Sean was strangely getting into Voodoo. He would put curses on people, and I wasn't sure how to respond to that craziness. My problem as a single mother was, I wanted to be married. He always had excuses and delays when it came to committing to marriage. His label was blowing up, Biggie dropped, and it was just about over. He also signed Mary J. Blige, and of course when I found out he slept with her, we fought. He claimed it was a mistake, and my stupid ass took him back, again. Sean asked me for a threesome with her, at first I was mad, but Mary was beautiful. It was our first threesome, and I loved it. Mary was sexy. I would not be doing this a lot, but it was so hot. I was young, and exploring my sexuality was enticing.

Over the years we brought other women into our bedroom periodically, and we were happy. That is until one day I came home to a situation that went from awkward to a nightmare. Quincy was with the babysitter, and Sean was sitting with Al B Sure at the dinner table. I had a child with Al, and Sean was the father in Quincy's life.
The awkwardness of all of us being together had dissolved a long time ago, but it was still weird that they were here, in my home, together, alone.

I sat down, and we had drinks. It was fun, the conversation was cool… until it wasn't. Al was a little loose after a couple of drinks. I remember him saying, "It's still weird seeing you with my friend, but you're happy, so I'm happy for you guys." Sean responded, "Thanks man. Me and you, we've shared so much." Al replied coolly, "Werd." The conversation took an odd and awkward turn when Sean said, "We all been together sexually but not together." I was shocked for a moment, as quietness lingered in the room, I asked "What do you mean by, all together." Al shifted uncomfortably, but Sean didn't hesitate, "You know how we sometimes invite other people into our bed." I couldn't believe it, "Oh hell no! Sean! This is my son's father! Al, say something!" What Al said was mind boggling. "I don't know. It could be kinda hot. I miss you in that way." Although I couldn't believe Sean would do this, the truth was, I still cared about Al, and this could be very hot. I just didn't want it messing up my relationship, and if things became awkward, how would it affect Quincy.

So I asked, "Are you both sure?" I imagined both of them inside of me. I knew this would be awkward sexually, there would be some bumping of genitals, but what happened next, I couldn't have imagined in my wildest dreams. Al xxxx xxxxx xxxxx xxxxxx. I couldn't believe it. I stood there in shock. But when Sean xxxxx xxxxx xxxxx xxxxx, I ran out of the room. This was too much. I couldn't. Sean called out to me, "Oh come on Kimmy!" They didn't chase after me. They xxxxx xxxxx xxxxxx.

I couldn't get the image out of my mind. I couldn't be with Sean for a while. But that wouldn't be the last time I saw Sean in a compromising position. Not by a long shot. One day I found the vault where he kept all of his encounters with men. Yes! He kept a record of it.

But that's for later.

# CHAPTER 6:
## PAC


Biggie took over East Coast Hip-Hop, and Sean was the brilliant mind that orchestrated it. He hired people to teach Chris how to flow and write his lyrics. He hired the best producers to do the beats (although he took credit for them), and the music was unstoppable. At this point Sean was sleeping with all the power players, and everyone that wanted to do music, wanted to be a Bad Boy. Sean wheeled-and-dealed in a way that would have been unthinkable to many. He slept with the guys that really controlled the music to stay on top. A lot of the names average people have never heard of. These are the guys that make the decisions on who is winning, and who is not. He hosted parties that were just a fancy name for orgies, and everyone wanted in.

When I met Tupac, Sean and I had an open relationship, and yes I slept with Pac. Shit, he was sexy. Sean didn't mind; well, not until he tried to get Pac to join both of us. Pac was not good with that. This is where the relationship between them became strained. Tupac wasn't going to accept Sean's advances. Pac wasn't gay, and he was pissed about the advances. We were all in Sean's house. I was drinking, they were smoking, and everyone was just relaxing. Sean came in on what I am sure he would call a smooth approach. "My baby is bad, isn't she?" Pac threw me a sly smile, "Hell yeah." I felt myself blush. Sean was now in full swing, "You think you hit it better than me?" I couldn't believe he disrespected me that way.

I was not playing with my response, "Sean! What the fuck?!" Pac came to my defense, "Damn bro, you ain't gotta do the sister that way!" Tupac appeared upset behind Sean's words, but Sean went in for the kill, regardless. "I think my dick's bigger than yours. I bet I can make her cum faster than you. What's up?" Pac was appalled. "What the fuck are you talking about, nigga? I ain't tryna run no fucking train." Sean continued, "What you scared of? Let's see who fucks better. Let her be the judge." Yes, at this point we had been inviting others into our bed for a while, but I am not used to, and will not stand for, disrespect. I wasn't the only one upset. Pac shouted, "Nigga, you talking about pulling your fucking dick out?" Sean was undaunted, "What you scared?" Tupac simply left.

Things were contentious since then. The two could not be in the same room. Pac avoided me as much as he did Sean. When they did bump into each other, the tension was palpable. It felt like blows could be thrown at any moment.

Months passed with only the tension between them. It was uncomfortable but nothing life or death, then one day while we were at the studio, it happened. I walked into Sean's office, and he was having, "The Conversation." Sean sat across from Jimmy Henchman, "Pac don't leave that fucking studio alive." I don't think I was supposed to hear it. I continued as if I didn't. "Hey Sean. Good morning, Jimmy." They didn't seem to think I heard anything. "I'm ordering breakfast." Smiling, Sean replied first, "Let me get eggs, sunny side up, with grits, and an orange juice." I could see he was hung over. Good. I don't want him knowing I know anything. If he just put a hit on

Pac, knowing something could be dangerous. Jimmy, apparently not hungry, said, "Nothing for me." As he stood to exit the room, he said to Sean, "Let's make that happen." Then nodded to me and said, "Kim, always a pleasure." With a wink to me, and a nod to Sean, he turned, and walked out. Jimmy was a part of our "intimate" circle. I went on as if nothing was happening. "I'll make the call now." I smiled as I left, hoping I wasn't white as a sheet.

I wasn't in the studio the night Pac survived being shot, thank God. From what I understand, Sean and Chris saw Pac at the studio after he'd been shot and did nothing. The way God works… After being shot, Pac made it to the elevator and tried to escape, but it stopped at the floor Sean and Chris were on. When the doors opened, they saw him lying on the elevator floor, riddled with bullets. The fact that they didn't call an ambulance, although they saw Pac lying there swimming in a pool of his own blood, would be all the evidence Pac ever needed. He of course assumed they placed the hit, and Tupac is a soldier, this is not something that will be unanswered. Tupac didn't do well. He lost a testicle. But he survived.

It was orchestrated, and Sean "Puffy" Combs,
was the orchestrator.

# CHAPTER 7:
# THREATS

At this point, I knew I had to get away from him, but I was scared. Is he going to take my life, if I try to escape? One February evening, I thought I found my opportunity at dinner, after an event. We were at a ritzy restaurant in a private booth. It was an exclusive setup, we were alone, but we were in public. Perfect! Sean was on the phone talking to an unknown listener as he sat down. His words on that call will be etched into my mind forever, "We're gonna release 'Who Shot Ya,' now." He waited for a response. Then went on to say, "Of course they gonna think B.I.G. was talking about Pac! That's the whole fucking point. Nobody would give a fuck about a diss track against L.L. fucking Cool J! Do you know how much money we'll make with this kinda rap beef? Niggas battling after someone really got shot!"

This may not be the best time for this conversation. Sean was finishing up, "We drop that shit tomorrow!" He listened into the phone then responded, "There's going to be blood in the street. Niggas missed, Pac's alive, let's capitalize on that shit. When he responds, it's just gonna mean, more money!" He turned around and looked at me. Spoke back into the phone, "I'll call you back." Then hung up and spoke to me. "What's wrong?" I tried my best to give a fake smile at what I'd heard. After all, me and Pac were intimate. I responded, "Nothing." Sean wasn't fooled. "Are you sure?" His demeanor was threatening, but I responded as cool as I could muster to his intimidating

stare, "Yeah of course." He took my hand saying, "That's wonderful." He began to squeeze my hand until it hurt as he continued, "Because seeing you walk in the office, while I was talking about killing that mother fucker, and you not saying shit to me, had me just a little concerned." His grip was starting to hurt, badly.
"You're hurting me." As he continued, he squeezed tighter, "You're pretending you didn't hear anything was a sign of your loyalty to me, not something I should be concerned with, right?" I had no choice but to give him the answer he wanted. I knew I was trapped when I responded, "Of course I'm loyal to you." He let me go as he responded, "Good. And remember, I'm the big dick."

I snatched my hand back in pain. He smiled and said, "Let's start off with a good wine." He snapped his fingers, and his favorite wine was poured for him. They knew what Sean wanted, and what he wanted he got. I'm trapped. Now isn't the time for me to launch my escape plan. I have to be strategic. It's going to be hard to leave the glamour, the glitz, the lifestyle, I mean this man just snapped his fingers in one of the most exclusive restaurants in New York City, and they poured his drink of choice. The bottle of wine is $800, and this is 1994. The list to get in this place is six months long if you are somebody. Mayor Giuliani has a table here tonight, also. If I got up and walked out, I would be safe, but what about tomorrow. I had to think. He sipped his wine and smiled. "You're not drinking?" He pointed at my glass, and of course a waiter filled it. They knew what I liked, as well.

Sean has a bad temper. He yells sometimes, and okay, he's roughed me up once or twice, but he never punched me, he never bruised me, and he never hit Quincy. I would not have stood for that. He never laid a hand on my son. At that time, I never thought of him touching Quincy in any way. Then the significance of what he said, hit me. Is he mad at Tupac, over me? 'I'm the big dick!' Oh my God. The last time he put his hands on me, it was because I enjoyed Jamie Foxx too much. Shit, he enjoyed Jamie too. He gets so insanely jealous. It's not fair. He wants to bring other men into the bedroom, but gets jealous when he does."Damn you're quiet tonight," he said snapping me back into the present. I asked the question that was burning in my mind since I walked into that office. "What does Chris think of this?" He looked at me coolly and said, "His fat ass better just keep doing music."

A third guest was escorted over by security. Sean motioned for him to sit. A waiter walked over to Sean Carter, and asked, "Would you like something?" Carter responded, "No thank you," then said, "Hello" to me with a smile. Smiling, I replied, "Hey Carter" and took a sip of my drink. The Seans may share a bed together from time to time, but thankfully, I was never asked to join. Carter went on to speak to Sean, "I thought we were meeting in private." Sean replied with a nonchalant shrug, "I had to discuss something with her. It's fine. Go ahead." He wielded this kind of power. Carter shifted uncomfortably in his chair before continuing, "It's true. Chris and Pac were about to start their own label." Sean slammed his fist against the table shouting, "Doesn't anyone have any fucking loyalty?" Carter, "Well that's not happening now, right?" Sean peered at Carter with distrust, "Why the fuck are you so eager to share this with me?

Chris is your man. Fuck, he brought you on, and you're stabbing him in the back?" Carter responded with indignity, "First, I'm tired of being that nigga's son, I need to come out from under his damn shadow." Sean smiled slightly, "Okay, I respect that." Carter kept going, "On top of that, this nigga is making that move, and it should have been with me!" Sean looked at Carter blankly, "Pac put Chris on. You know this. What's this really all about, Carter? Don't fucking try to play me." The Jay-Z of today wasn't born yet, this young Sean Carter was in over his head. Cornered, he had to spill it out. "I want his spot." "Ambition. Now this is a man I can work with." Sean made a grandiose gesture toward Carter. "Waiter, get this mother fucker whatever he wants." Carter smiled, "Thank you." Sean responded, "Honesty and ambition. We're gonna make a lot of bread together." Carter ordered a drink, as he stated again, "Guess he won't be leaving with that nigga to do their own label now." Sean responded with his normal air of arrogance, "Why don't you let me worry about that."

I took this as my cue to escape. I told Sean, "I'm going to go ahead and get back to Quincy." Sean was wrapped up in his conversation with Carter, and barely noticed as he excused me, "Have the limo drop you off."

We didn't eat. He didn't care.
I smiled and kissed him on the cheek and left.

CHAPTER 8:
KIDADA

Actress, model and fashion designer, Kidada Jones, was
Tupac Shakur's fiancé, and is the daughter of record
producer, Quincy Jones, and actress Peggy Lipton. Being
around other celebrities was just a part of life. Meeting
Kidada was just one of those events, and as time went on,
we became close. We hung out together, went shopping,
and so on. It was about the same time I met Kimora. Those
were the days, or so I thought. We always had girl talk, and
the fact she was dating someone I had previously been with
wasn't a source of contention. We didn't get jealous of each
other. It was just girl talk stuff. No, I did not become
intimate with Kidada, Kimora was too jealous for that.
Yes, Kidada knew about Kimora, Sean, and I, all being
together sexually. Of course she did. We shared that kind of
thing. We were open and honest with each other about
almost everything. A true friendship except, I couldn't be
open and honest about, everything. Not anymore. Sean
made sure of that.

     Kidada and Pac were the greatest couple. He was
always so cool, and yes sexy. She was so beautiful and fun.
Before all the tension and beef, we used to all hang out
together, it was always dope vibes. But with Pac's shooting,
and the suspicions surrounding Sean and Jimmy, the vibes
between Kidada and I weren't always perfect.

     Then came that night. Award shows weren't
anything new for us, at this point. We dolled up as the men

groomed. We didn't choose what we wore, a stylist prepared our color pallets, a make-up artist did our make-up, and a hair stylist did our hair. This was just the way of things. We shared the best stylists in the business. Sometimes we would all go to the studio for an event to get our measurements taken, but this time, Kidada seemed different. I felt like something was wrong, but when I probed her, she wouldn't say anything.

Then the day of the event was here. We would all see each other inside. Even though Sean was my man, as far as props, I had nothing on Kidada. Being Quincy Jones' daughter had perks, and superstardom was among them. Pac wasn't there. When she saw us, she came over to our table. We sat around kicking it in a very dope vibe. Sean knew he was going to clean up this award show. He had all but taken over the East Coast, musically. With all the hits, there really was no way he wouldn't. Bad Boy is hall of fame stuff now, and Sean "P. Diddy" Combs knew it.

Sean smiled at Kidada as she sat at our table, but something about that smile didn't seem authentic. Soon I would know why. He's sick when he has a grudge against someone. As she sat Sean said, "Bad Boy is going to clean the fuck up!" From his table with Faith, Chris replied, "Hell yeah! And that new shit we bustin' out, gonna have these niggas sick." Kidada signaled for the waiter to pour her a glass of the ginger-ale that sat over at her table. As the waiter refreshed her drink she said, "Pac's music gonna get some love too." Sean grimaced. "Oh come on Sean, I know y'all got your differences, but you have to admit, the man makes great music." Sean looked at me out the corner of his eye, then took another sip of his favorite cognac, and replied, "Bad Boy got the hottest music on the fucking planet. But I ain't tripping, everybody gotta get their shine, right?"

Kidada sighed, "Sean, Tupac thinks you were involved with him getting shot. You two were so close. You need to make this right." Sean responded indignantly, "Why the fuck would that nigga think I had anything to do with it?" Kidada retorted, "Sean, can you blame him?" Sean was obviously not happy with that question by his reply, "Hell yeah, I blame him, we had a good thing going. All of us. That nigga turned on me, and he has the fucking balls to blame me for his shooting?" The indignity he managed to spew out while lying through his teeth was something I did not expect. I was thrown back for a moment before interjecting, "Da, do we have to do this tonight? It's Sean's big night." Kimora heard the ruckus and made her way over to our table as well. She sat down and said, "Hey everybody," with that big, dimpled smile. I smiled, and replied, "Hey!" Kidada also seemed happy to see her as she said, "Hey, what up, Kimmy?" Kimora, never the type to hold her tongue went straight at it, "The whole place is buzzing with the fact you're sitting here accusing Sean of having Pac shot. Ya'll kinda… uh loud." She laughed. Kidada seemed embarrassed as she looked around to see everybody staring and whispering. But she wasn't about to back off. In fact, she doubled down, "Anybody here not talking about it, ain't real anyway. We all know Sean was behind it." Kimora forced a smile, "Honey we don't have to do this here." Kidada made clear she was not to be silenced as she continued, "Oh let's not hurt the feelings of Sean "Puffy" Combs. He only had one

of the most prolific rappers in the game shot."
Sean clenched his hands into fists. If this was anyone else, this would have turned ugly. But this was Quincy Jones' daughter. Sean was a monster in the streets, well feared by men that knew, but he did not want any of the smoke Quincy Jones could bring. Kidada could continue with impunity. Sean could not touch her. Christopher and Mary, both wanting to defend the super producer that made them famous, both started to stand, and make their way over to the table. But Sean signaled them off, with a firm motion of his hand. They remained in their seats watching helplessly.

Kidada seemed to be on a full rampage, "You're not safe in the streets Sean. You think you're untouchable?" Kimora seemed almost red in the face, when she grabbed Kidada by the hand saying, "I gotta go to the rest room." Kidada not willing to stop, snatched her hand away yelling, "Let go of me!" Kimora needed her to get a grip and said sternly as a parent speaking to a child mid-tantrum, "Da!" Kidada turned to her and yelled, "What!" Kimora nodded toward the crowded room, and Kidada looked around. Here she deflated slightly. Kimora now in control, spoke firm but softly, "Let's go powder our nose!" Kidada nodded with a grimace and gave a sharp look back at Sean as she walked away.

As attention slowly melted away, I asked Sean, "You okay?" Sean didn't reply at first. He looked around, saw that no one was really paying attention now that the ruckus had died down, and stood to get the pitcher of ginger-ale from Kidada's table. He poured himself a drink from it, looked around again, saw no one was paying attention, and put the pitcher under the table. What was he doing? Then I heard the distinct sound of liquid being poured into liquid. Oh my God. Is he… Peeing in the pitcher? He smiled at me as he brought the pitcher back from under the table, and finally replied to me, "I'm good." He then stood and returned the pitcher to the table. I was in awe. I knew he had a bad temper, but this was disgusting. I'll never eat or drink something after we have an argument again.

Kidada and Kimora made their way back to Kidada's table to sit, as Sean watched on quietly. Sean made small talk. "Which songs do you think they'll give me awards for?" As Kidada poured her drink, Sean's bodyguard made his way over to the table. I think he stopped her from drinking, as everyone else just sat and watched. Gene risked incurring Sean's wrath, if I'm right. Relieved I replied, "Babe your catalogue is crazy. It could be a lot of songs."

Sean glared at Kidada's table the entire night.

## CHAPTER 9:
## GOING BACK TO CALI

We had a wild night, it was after one of Sean's infamous parties. Everyone was there, and we not only had threesomes, but we also swapped partners. Our sex life was crazy, but I got to do things with Sean I would never have been able to do with a straight man. Sean cared about me, but it was becoming more and more obvious that he preferred men. I was beginning to think I was there more to cover his wild desires, than because he really wanted to be with me. He was like Caesar, every woman's man, and every man's woman. But truthfully, at that stage, I was becoming okay with it.

I woke up and left the bedroom where I was with Jada Pinkett, and Sean happened to be coming out of the bedroom with Xxxxx, and Will Smith. Yes, Xxxxx attended the parties from time to time. I could see him and Will kind of snuggled up on the bed together. I was grateful I wasn't asked to join in that room. I didn't really like Xxxxx. Sean smiled when he saw me, "Good morning." Here at the orgies, he wasn't very affectionate. He didn't have to pretend, but he couldn't walk straight. I knew how his ass felt, literally. We've had sessions playing with each other's anal cavities.

I wanted to be home before Quincy woke up, so I told him, "I'm getting ready to go." He responded, "Let's have a cup of coffee first." This meant he wanted to talk.

I didn't know what it was about, but in situations like this, I didn't really have a choice. He was becoming more violent when he didn't get what he wanted, and I didn't really want to fight. So, I sat down. But before we started talking, Xxxxx came out of the room. Sean was wearing boxers; Xxxx was in his birthday suit. Xxxxx addressed us, "Morning." When he turned around, in order to close the door, there was a dried cum stain on his back. Xxxxx walked over, pulled a chair out to sit down next to us, and lit up a blunt. Sean stretched, smiled, and said, "This East Coast-West Coast, beef is more lucrative than I thought, but it's getting dangerous." Xxxxx responded surprised. "Business first thing in the morning? Damn cuz, you on it. But you know you don't got nothing to worry about. You got a pass, daddy." Xxxxx smiled coyly. Sean apparently had something to talk about with Xxxxx as well, because he said, "I can't protect everybody. Especially if someone is no longer going to be on my label." It was apparent Xxxx was taken aback by this turn of events by his reply, "Sean, are you saying what I think your saying?" Sean continued, "It's taxing on my resources to protect people. Someone that isn't 100% on my team, can't get 100% of my protection."

What the hell is going on here? What did Sean want from me? This morning is turning out to be way more than I expected, and I have to go, Quincy will be looking for me. Meanwhile, Xxxx apparently wanted clarity. "So, to be clear, if something happened," Xxxxx made quotation marks with his fingers, "to one of your artists, that was leaving your label anyway, it would be considered," he makes another set of quotation marks, "out of your control.

Is that what you're saying?" Wait a minute, can they be talking about Biggie? Is Sean saying he won't protect Biggie? At this point I was too young, too naïve, too hung over, to understand that this was not a lack of protection, this was a hit. Where did this come from this morning? But an older, wiser me, understands now what I did not comprehend all those years ago. Sean was just getting to the real reason that he had Xxxx there. The world was about to lose Biggie. Xxxxx laughed, "You a cold motherfucker." Sean said, "Why the fuck should I protect someone that isn't gonna stick around. I made him. That nigga should be worshipping the ground I fucking walk on." I was thinking 'Sean's ego is rearing its ugly head,' and I wanted to get out of there, but instincts told me, I need to tread carefully. So, my next move had to be calculated. I don't really want any part of this. Not even implicitly. But, I was just dragged right into the middle of it. If what was happening here ever comes out, will I be held as an accomplice? But even as those thoughts crossed my mind, I couldn't just pretend this was okay, so I said, "But Sean, he hasn't left yet. They're just rumors. Are you going to let him die because of some rumors?"

Sean glared at me, the anger in his voice obviously stemming from hurt as he said, "I know when I'm being betrayed. I am not killing anyone. But I am NOT protecting somebody that doesn't have my back 150%. Fuck that!" This was railing out of control. My mind began to race. Is there a way to get through to him? Maybe I could use the finance route, "Sean, he's bringing in so much money. You put so much money into cultivating him. Are you going to throw away all that money?" That's when he revealed how 'thought out' this meeting really was. "If he leaves, he takes all the money I invested into creating him." Sean sighs, "But, if he can't protect himself, and something terrible does happen, then the money I would make off of his death would blow away all the money we made so far." I was perplexed, "Sean…" He continued, "He's worth more to me dead than alive." Sean Combs is a calculated monster. Xxxx chimes in, "I get that fam. A lot of people out there want Biggie dead, too. Without your protection, he doesn't stand a chance in Cali." Biggie is going to die. This is crazy. I dare not say anything else about it.

Sean smiles and stands to walk over to a safe behind a picture. There he pulls out a bag marked with Xxxx's name. He turns to Xxxx and says, "That's why you're worth your weight in gold. You understand me. Here's a little something for you to take care of my people." Xxxx smiles, "Sean, I love you baby. You know I got your back. Your problems are my problems. I'll make sure to have my people take care of your people."

I need to get out of here, this is crazy, I attempted to leave again. "Sean, I want to get to Quincy before he wakes up. Sean looked at me responding, "It's getting late. Give him a kiss from me." I'm going to get out of here. Thank God. Xxxx, always with something to say, "I'd love to meet the little tike sometime." Not a chance in hell. Something about this guy creeps me out. I forced a smile, "That would be great."

I made my exit.

# CHAPTER 10:
## THE LIES YOU TELL

At this point, the relationship between Sean and I had been off-and-on for quite a while, and we were off at this point. He had put his hands on me again, this time, for something that didn't even happen. It was all in his head. When the phone rang, I picked it up anyway. "Hi, Sean." He sounded trepidatious, as he said, "We been broken up for a while this time." "Yeah." He continued, "I don't want anyone to know about my," he paused to search for the right word. "Proclivities?" I replied, "So you don't want people to know about you being gay."

Sean exploded, "See, that's why I fucking lose control on you!" So, I just plainly stated, "Goodbye Sean." "Wait!", he screamed. "What Sean?" "I'm sorry, okay?!." "You're always fucking sorry!" He took a deep breath. "I have to do something to cover myself." I sighed, "Do whatever you fucking want, Sean." "When you see this in the news, it's… it's not real." This made me calm down a moment. What could he be talking about. He continued, "I'm only doing it for the press." "Doing what Sean?" After a long pause he continued. "She knows what this is. She is just pretending to cover me." "Sean, what the hell are you talking about?" Another pause, "Publicly, I am going to be dating someone else. A video girl." I laughed, "Why would you do that?" "I have to cover myself." I was getting mad. I was actually angrier at myself more than at him. Why was I getting jealous?

I was sitting there actually comparing myself to video vixens in my mind. They are thick but look at my body. Did he prefer them light skinned big butt girls from videos?

I calmed myself. No, I know he likes men, any damned way. As I regained control I asked, "Why the hell are you telling me?" He sighed, "I wanted you to find out from me, first." "Like I give a shit!" He came at me with his favorite line, "You know I love you." It was getting old. I could only think to myself, 'here we go.' Love is a big, strong word. I'm tired of him throwing it around and using it when it fits his needs. He's using it while he's sitting here telling me about dating someone else. I replied, "You don't hit people you love Sean. Love doesn't hurt." He sucked his teeth as he responded, "Come on, are you serious? That shit's for children. We aren't in fucking high school. Sometimes things happen. That doesn't mean I don't love you. I wouldn't hit you if I didn't. Wait. Wait. That sounded wrong." "You said exactly what you meant."

He took a breath. There was an awkward silence. The fact I was still on the phone and waiting for him to speak meant he had the power. He was more cautious as he continued. He didn't want to lose that power. "Kim, no one that I don't care about can bring that kind of emotion out of me." I wanted to say, 'Is that how you talk to dudes after using butt plugs?', but there is a line I dare not cross. Instead I said, "You say that while you're dating some other bitch!" "That's just for the public." I was done. It could be heard in my voice as I said, "Whatever Sean. Do what you need to do, leave me alone. "I'm never giving up on us.", he cried. I responded to that emotional control attempt with the little resolve I could muster. I didn't even believe the words that came tumbling out of my mouth. "Sean there is no 'us' anymore. Goodbye." "Tell Quincy I miss him.", he threw out. His emotional manipulation was really driving me crazy. This time I said with much more conviction, "Goodbye Sean.". I hung up.

Manipulative bastard.

# CHAPTER 11:
## MO' PROBLEMS

For a while, I was actually happy to see Sean gone. I was getting' older, and the sex parties were out of control. It was getting time for me to slow down. Quincy was getting older. I knew that if I kept going, the rumors circulating were going to eventually find a way to get back to him. What will he think of me? Chris is about to take his trip to California. I didn't know exactly what was going to happen out there, but I felt like T'yanna Wallace was about to be an orphan. I knew I didn't want any ties to that.

As I was sitting there contemplating all of this in my robe, sipping my wine on this Friday evening, my doorbell rings. I was not expecting company. I opened the door, and found Sean. My heart skipped a beat. I was shocked but recovered quickly. I forced a smile, and told him with a slightly slurred speech, "Hey, come on in." Shit, I am way more intoxicated than I thought. Sean entered looking around suspiciously. Then turned to me and smiled saying, "You haven't been returning my calls. I just wanted to make sure you're okay." "I'm fine." He obviously was not here out of, 'concern.' He was checking to see who was here. Sean was controlling like that. Yes, even though we were not together, and he was dating someone else. He started to make his way to the living room. I attempted to put a quick end to the visit, but it came out a little more directly than I intended, "So, since you can see I'm fine, you can let me go to bed now." Part of me wanted him to stay. As he entered the living room, I was forced to follow, Sean was very direct with his next inquiry, "Is someone else waiting for you?" "No but, Sean, we're not together. You're dating someone else. I can fuck whoever I choose." With this Sean became irate. He fiercely slammed me to the ground. Then he pulled out a 22. and sat it on the end table. He turned to me calmly. I was scared. My voice quivered as I plead to him, "Sean please stop. Quincy is here."

How did we get here? How did we get to the point that he was in my living room, threatening me with a gun? He knelt on one knee, and got right in my face to say, "You're mine. You don't have a choice in that now. I can't live without you." He stood up composing himself. I was terrified as I whimpered, "Sean, that's not love." Sean picked up his gun and cocked it. He looked at me almost thoughtfully and asked, "Have you ever heard, 'if I can't have you, no one can'." "Sean please don't. Please. Quincy will hear." Sean smiled, and put the gun away saying, "Oh this is just for dramatic effect. I would never shoot you. If I was going to kill you, no one will trace it to me. You know how many people I've had to take care of over the years. It would be quiet. Something in your food, or drink. Something that will never get back to me. I wouldn't shoot you. Do you understand?" I could only nod, tears flowing down my cheeks. He looked at me thoughtfully. As he reached down to help me up, I could do nothing but agree. He's a terrifying monster.

Now, he wanted to smooth it over, and I had to go along with it. What else could I do? "Listen baby, I don't ever want to hurt you. You know I really love you, or I would have moved on. Thinking about living my life without you is just too hard. If someone ever tried to hurt you, I would kill them." My back hurt, from where I hit it on the table, when he shoved me. All I could do as he helped me up was nod that I understood through my streaming tears, which he wiped. He looked toward Quincy's room, "Let me say goodnight." "No Sean, please, he…" thinking quickly, "He has to get up in the morning." Sean looked at me with an unreadable look, he was studying me. "Okay. I'm gonna go." Nervously, I walked him to the front door. This is over. Thank God. He kissed me. I didn't want him touching me, but I couldn't refuse. "Kiss Quincy for me." I tried to keep my composure as I replied. "Sure Sean." He opened the door to leave, the bodyguard that was waiting outside escorted him to the car. This was far worse than I realized. Why would he need a bodyguard, at my front door? How was he anticipating this to go? After I shut the door, I had another drink. For tonight the nightmare was over. I sipped on my wine and cried.

The next few days he sent dozens of flowers. He brought Quincy expensive toys. He didn't want me, he wanted me to keep his secret. I'm trapped. He has the authorities under his thumb, I can't go to them. This is like a gangster movie. How high up does his power go? How far is his reach? The FBI? The CIA? Who is not corrupted, or won't get silenced by their upper chain of command? Can anyone help me and my child?

He found his way back to my bed. I had no choice.

# CHAPTER 12:
## A MAMA'S LOVE

The calamity that ensued behind the death of Biggie shook the East Coast. It rocked me as well. Sean could have stopped it. He was complicit in it. He was a contributor. He knew it was going to happen and didn't stop it. This was his friend. No, they were not nearly as close as Sean would have the public believe, but still.

As far as Sean was concerned, we were great. To the public, we were just having the off-and-on relationship of a normal couple, and I probably just seemed like a money-hungry hoe. But the truth is, I just got used to not having a choice. Today, I recognized it for what it was, Stockholm Syndrome. I was at his beck-and-call, and had become comfortable with it. Quincy had everything he could ever want, with the exception of course, of a normal parental figure. That is why this chapter is so powerful for me. A mother's love is so real.

One night I was out with my, "boyfriend," (yes, we were on again), and we were joined for dinner by none other than Ms. Wallace. Sean looked over, as security allowed Ms. Wallace to approach the table and sit. Ms. Wallace spoke with a smile, "Hello Sean, hi Kim." I smiled the best I could. What a situation. For all intents and purposes, she is sitting with her son's killer. I hope my voice didn't betray my feelings as I said,"Hi, Ms. Wallace." Sean smiled also, as he said, "Hello Ms. Wallace. What can

I do for you? When I got your call, it sounded urgent."
He was able to appear as if he was smiling warmly.

This was the creepiest situation of my entire life. She looked at Sean with pleading eyes, "I know this isn't your problem. But things have gotten kind of hard. I was hoping that you could send some of that money Chris made with you, this way." Sean shook his head. "That's not something I can just do. There are attorneys, and accountants. Can I maybe help you out with a little something to get you past the hump?" Sean reached into his pocket to dig for his wallet. "I haven't even seen how much Chris left. It's going on two years. Just how long is this going to take?" Sean sighed as he replied, "These things are difficult Mrs. Wallace. I don't know. The attorneys don't make this easy."

Ms. Wallace pushed further, "I don't understand what's so difficult. He worked for you. He made his money. Where is it?" Sean shook his head as if saddened by what he was saying as he continued, "It's not like I can just give you, his money. You're entitled to certain amounts, and they are just trying to figure out what that amount is. I don't mean to sound cruel, but it wouldn't be fair to me, to just give you tons of money." "You got rich off my son, and now you're keeping all of his money!" Sean kept his cool as he replied, "I'm afraid business isn't that cut and dry, Ms. Wallace. I paid for publishing, publicity, I mean in all actuality, if I am going to be straight forward, Mrs. Wallace, Chris probably owed me money. I won't know until it's all worked out."

The anger in Ms. Wallace's voice barely overshadowed the pain, or perhaps it magnified it as she uttered the only words she could muster, "You bastard." Sean didn't flinch. He just said, "Look at the contract. I am honestly trying to get him as much as possible out of it, but I have investors. I can't just take money that doesn't belong to him and start giving it away." Ms. Wallace exploded in response, "You know good and well, Chris didn't owe you a damned thing!" Sean stared her straight in the eye unwaveringly and said, "He would have started making a profit after a few years. His money, until his album sales paid for studio time, music videos, publishing, and marketing, would have come from doing shows. I'm sorry, he isn't here to make that money. I miss him." Her response was dead pan, "Did you kill my son?" Momentarily, Sean was stunned into silence. She asked again, her voice quivering, "Did you?" He started, "Ms. Wallace…" She would not be redirected, "Answer the question!" I was not used to seeing Sean on the defensive. "No! Of course not." She looked at him with spite, the anger in her voice enough to send shivers up my spine, as she replied with a menace only a mother can, "I don't believe you Sean." Sean looked at her with a sadness that I knew in my soul to be fake, although looking at him without context, anyone would believe him, as he replied, "I'm sorry to hear that."

Today I know he was able to muster that false sincerity, because he's a sociopath. Back then, I thought it was compassion. With no more words, Ms. Wallace stood up and left. Sean watched her exit with disbelief. Not knowing what to do, I placed my order. Dinner that night was long, and silent. I feared for Ms. Wallace's life. Sean is most dangerous when he feels threatened.

No, she could not physically threaten him, but this threat was very real. If she goes public with her accusations, Sean's image would be damaged.

I have felt for myself the extents he will go through,
in order to protect that image.

# CHAPTER 13:
## HAVE SOME FAITH

The fact of the matter is, Sean was a complete control freak. He was absolutely the worst. But of all the things he did for control, this might have been one of the most despicable ones. We were in the Bad Boy office one evening, sitting in the lounge area, enjoying a meal. Sean was smoking one of those big cigars he liked, when Faith entered, and sat down with us. She seemed relaxed as she said, "Hey guys." I smiled. I never had any bad vibe from the marvelous, Faith Evans. We never talked about the wild time the three of us shared at one of Sean's parties. I gave her a hug, "Hey girl. What's up?" Sean smiled and asked, "Hey. What brings you out?" She addressed Sean saying, "Look, when you asked me to hook up with Chris, I understood. You needed to control him. I felt honored that you would choose me to 'monitor' one of your most valuable assets. Chris is sweet. Sean laughed and said, "Honestly. I knew you would be good. Make the big man feel loved." "I don't feel good about all this Sean." Sean got that look in his eye he gets before he blows his top. Faith saw it also. She treaded carefully, "Sean, you know I'm as loyal as they come."

Sean leaned forward unintentionally threatening and said in a low tone, "Yeah?" "But Sean, Chris and I had a child together." Sean leaned back. He let out a deep breath. "I'm gonna take care of you. You're not like Chris. You're loyal." Faith had a tear in her eye as she responded,

"He didn't have to die." This is getting very touchy. Did she know? Did she suspect? Was this her trying to find out, if Sean intentionally killed Biggie? I wanted to ask, but of course there was no way of doing that. This is so crazy. Sean sighed and replied, "He didn't. Don't get me wrong. I miss him. But he was leaving me anyway. No one cares about my pain." Classic narcissistic Sean. It's all about him. I was sickened for a moment. But his next sentence made me feel for him anyway. "I wanted to share all this with him. He was my man." Faith couldn't hide the anger that flared in her eyes, but she knew who she was talking to. She was careful as she spoke. "Sean, you have your friends you share things with." Sean sat forward again, this time with malicious intention as he queried, "What the fuck is that supposed to mean?" "Chris had no one. Only you." Sean lost it. "That fat fuck, and that other piece of shit I had you fuck,,," I interjected while in shock, "You had her fuck Pac?" Sean glared at me as he answered, "Yes, fucking Pac. Those motherfuckers were going to try to start their own label and compete with me! Me! Me!! After all I did for that fat fuck! Nah, I wasn't using resources to protect that mother fucker. No fucking way!" As Faith started to cry, Sean looked at her, and softened slightly. He spoke a little calmer. "Look I didn't hate him. I was hurt. But I didn't hate him. I'll make sure you and C.J. are taken care of."

Without words, Faith got up to leave. As she turned, Sean spoke softly, "Faith?" She ignored him. He called to her again, "Faith?" She exited quickly. Sean just looked at me and said, "Damn!" I really didn't know what to say. Sean just told Faith that he wouldn't protect her husband, because he was going to leave Bad Boy. From a business perspective, I didn't disagree with Sean there. If you're leaving, and creating competition for him, why would he spend resources on you. So, I hugged Sean. But I also knew he didn't have to send Chris to California. I wondered if he realized that he sentenced him to death? He hugged me back with tears in his eyes as he asked, "How the fuck am I the bad guy? Huh? I fucking do nothing but bust my ass to make everyone live comfortably, and I'm supposed to just let niggas walk all over me?" As I held him in a comforting embrace, I replied, "No baby." He took me right there on the couch.

Like I said, 'Stockholm Syndrome.'

CHAPTER 14:
OUT SHYNE


This particular evening, I was at Sean's house, and Quincy was staying with a friend. It was some alone time for Sean and I, until the doorbell rang, and Sean got up to answer it. I heard a woman yelling, and quickly realized that is was Jennifer Lopez, or better known to the world as, 'J.Lo'.

"Sean, what the fuck?!", she blasted. Sean responded calmly, "Relax, baby!" "Why the hell did you have to start shooting? Isn't that what we have bodyguards for?" Normally when these kinds of situations arise, I remain quiet, and just listen. I play my position you could say, but I wasn't paying attention to the news for the last day or so, and even though it would be the only thing anyone would talk to me about for months, no one had spoken to me about it yet. So, I entered the foyer asking, "What's going on?" Jennifer exploded at me, "What's going on? What's going on? This nigga  shot up a damn club." My jaw dropped looking back and forth between the two. Sean spoke soothingly, "Jen, you gotta calm down." Jennifer was having none of it. She continued, "Calm down? Calm down?! You shot a bunch of innocent people, Sean!" Sean placed his hand on her forearm. It's a bonding technique. He was shrewd in handling her. He does this to me, too. Even if you know what's happening it works. It's an intimate contact without being personal. He was aiming to disarm her. This did not seem to immediately sway Jennifer as she continued, "Why in the hell do you think Biggie's replacement will take the fall for you." Biggie's replacement? Wait, could she be talking about… I had to know, "Are you talking about Shyne?" Jennifer didn't even look at me as she responded, "Yes, fucking Shyne!" Sean continued with a calm and even voice, "Relax. The situation is under control." Jennifer was not calming down. She went on, "They contacted my attorney for my statement, and there are a lot of witnesses, Sean! There is no way you're going to get away with this."

Sean's arrogance can be immeasurable at times. He laughed as he asked, "You doubting me?" I couldn't believe it. I had to know, "Sean, what could you offer him that would make him do a bid for you. Like what the fuck?" Jennifer also remarked, "And what if he falters halfway through his sentence and starts talking." Sean responded as calmly as ever, "He won't do that. People in jail don't cross connected people on the outside." Jennifer looked deflated, "So, you'll kill him too?" How much does she know? "Look, I'm not going to threaten anyone. Shyne is smart and loyal. He knows how it works, and when he gets out, he'll be well taken care of." Jennifer spoke defiantly, "Sean, they want to question me. I am not perjuring myself. I am not going to jail over this." Sean seemed so in control; I admired him for it at this point, but my spirit was broken.

I felt bad for Jennifer. She catches one bad break after another, and this was a really bad break. Sean spoke with confidence, "Relax. Come in and have a drink. Have your lawyers call mine. You'll never see the witness stand.

I promise." Jennifer wasn't so sure. She asked him, "How can you possibly know that?" Sean smiled as he replied, "Between Shyne's confession, and the witnesses that gave their accounts, the cops won't need much else. The statement from your lawyer will be fine." Jennifer's next concern popped up. She explained, "My attorney? Sean, he's good, but he won't do this." Beaming with confidence, the way only a man with his net worth can, Sean responded, "Sure, he will." Jennifer shook her head defiantly as she responded. "Sean, you don't know him." Sean's unbreakable confidence was ruling the day. Jennifer was giving in as he told her with a smile, "I got this." "Sean, are you sure?" Sean gave a wink, "My attorneys handle situations. Give him my number too." Jennifer seemed leery as she asked, "You're not going to threaten my attorney?" Sean laughed as he replied, "No. Of course not. Money talks baby." He turned to me and said, "Take her inside, and pour her a drink." I had question of my own, "But, you were going to make Shyne the label's go-to-man. What are you gonna do now?" Sean looked disappointed as he responded, "He had the voice, but his flow…" He sighed, "Well, artists with his talent, are a dime a dozen." Looking at Jen he continued, "He's not a once-in-a-lifetime find like Jennifer Lopez," Now he's throwing on the charm. Despite the situation, she blushed slightly. Sean continued, "Let's grab that drink. Let me handle this attorney situation. Relax. Don't worry."

We left the foyer and went to have a seat in the living room. He tried to make a threesome happen that night. It didn't work out.

Not that day.

# CHAPTER 15:
## QUEEN BITCH

Kimora Simmons and I went out to have drinks. She was looking at me seductively, and I was turned on. We were gonna go back to my place afterwards, but suddenly after a sip of my drink, I felt like I had to vomit. I excused myself, and barely made it to the lady's room. When I came back, Kimora asked, "You feeling okay?" "I'm fine. I have been under the weather the last couple of days. I think I'll head home." She said, "Your breasts are looking kinda plump there, girl." Embarrassed I whispered, "Not in public." She replied simply, "Are you pregnant?!" I was taken completely aback. "Why the hell would you say that?" She let it sit there for a minute. I bet in her head she was like, 'Wait for it, wait for it'. Then it hit me… "Shit!" She gave me a minute before continuing, "So what 'ya gonna do?" I didn't understand. "Gonna do?" "If it's not Sean's? Fuck. If it is?" With the shock wearing off, the scope of the situation began to take hold. I responded, "I better get a test."

She looked at me with pity, "Damn girl. Good luck. After what he did to Chris, I wouldn't want to be in your shoes." The desire that was in her eyes before I got sick, was all but gone. As I began to stand, I realized what she said to me, and I paused. She looked at me flatly and said, "Ain't nobody stupid, girl." I didn't know what to say. The question still lingered in my mind despite everything I knew, 'Did Puffy intentionally kill Chris?' She brought me back to the moment by saying, "Go." Not knowing what else to say, but knowing I had to deal with my situation right now, I replied, "I-I'll hit you up."

She sighed and simply repeated, "Good luck."

# CHAPTER 16:
# CHRISTIAN

The next day I was sitting on my couch deep in thought, when my doorbell rang. I went to let Sean in. This was going to be scary. We made our way back to the living room and we sat down. Quincy was asleep. Sean seemed legitimately concerned. "What's so urgent?" I didn't know what else to do. I just blurted it out. "I'm pregnant." The air in the room was as thick as J.Lo.

He was quiet. What is he thinking? He asked the obvious question, "Are you sure?" I spoke rapidly, "I was on the pill. I'll get rid of it. I'm sorry. I just wanted you to know." "That's wonderful! This is great?" I was so confused. "Huh? You're… You're not mad." He laughed, "Mad? No. Why would I be mad at this wonderful news? I'm gonna be a dad, with the woman I love bearing my child. What could possibly be better?" He jumped right on the phone and called one of his besties. I could hear Will Smith congratulating him. Sean said, "Yeah. Definitely. Hold on. Kim, baby." I was still in awe of the fact that he didn't get angry, and yes I will admit, I was sure he was going to hit me. So, it was with relief when I replied, "Yes?" He told me excitedly, "We gotta have a party." His excitement was contagious. I was getting really excited too, "Yes, a gender reveal and…" He cut me off. "Yes, of course we're doing all of that but, everyone is going to want to sleep with you right before you give birth." My heart sank in my chest. "Everybody is going to want to what?!" Sean went on with the same excitement, "Well, not everybody, you know, Will, Jada, Xxxxx…" "Sean, I'm having your baby." He verbally waived me off. "It'll be fine!" I couldn't help myself, I just started crying. Sean grew quiet on the phone. Then spoke low, "I'll call you back." He hung up and took me by the hand. "Baby, I never ask anything from you." I tried to see him through the tears streaming down my face. I couldn't believe the words coming out of his mouth. I tried to speak, "Sean…" He cut me off, "I provide everything anyone could ever want. Do you want for anything?" Sobbing I replied, "No but…" He continued, "This is the kind of thing I have to do in order to continue giving you this comfortable lifestyle, where you live in the lap of luxury, and get to be on TV shows, and in movies. I know you don't want this, but do you want all of this to go away?" A whimper is all I could manage, "No." He continued softly, "Then we gotta do this?" I said, "But Sean, I don't believe in all this spiritual crazy shit. We got here because you're brilliant. Not because of the sex parties." He replied, "Do you trust me?" I did. My soul was so broken, I did. I responded, "Yes." He sighed as he said, "Then let's do what we need to do, to keep what we have." As I nodded yes, he pulled me in to hug me, "Thank you baby. We are going to have a beautiful baby."

He ordered me some food, and that night, I cried myself to sleep. I was going to be gang-banged at nine months pregnant? I want my children out of this life. My child's going to have a good, Biblical name. A heavy, Christian name.

They are not going to take his soul….

## CHAPTER 17:
## BROKEN PROMISES

I don't know how this managed to stay out of the media for so long, but Sean got to the point where he was incredibly abusive, and only his inner circle knew about it. The artists were all too afraid of him to say anything. He had gained so much power. No one would say anything. Puff Daddy was a Kingpin.

This Monday afternoon, Quincy was in school, and our son Christian was with the nanny, and I still had to make a living. I still loved the camera and had just been cast for a new movie. Sean was coming over to celebrate with me. Just the two of us. I was in the bathroom when he came in. We were supposed to go out for dinner, but he was in a foul mood. Sean yelled, "What the fuck!" I would have to walk on eggshells as I came out of the bathroom, but I found him holding flowers, so I smiled, "You brought me flowers!" Sean yelled, "No! So who the fuck are they from?" I was bewildered, and told him honestly, "I don't know. Probably just a fan."

He threw the attached card at me. I picked it up to read it. "Sean I…" He slapped me so hard I hit the ground. Sean yelled, "Who the fuck were you with the other night?" I looked down at the card that was lying on the ground next to me, and it read, 'The other night was amazing, we must do it again.' Shit. I tried to explain, "Sean…" He threw the flowers at me. "That's not how this works! You have my child! You don't touch anyone, unless I allow it!" I yelled

back, "It was just coffee with the producer, it was nothing!"
He glared at me, and asked, "Who the fuck is this
producer?" I was trying desperately to calm him down, as I
responded, "From the movie, babe! Calm down!" He
picked up my coffee mug and slammed it against the wall.
Coffee flew everywhere as he yelled, "Who the fuck this
nigga think he is?" "Sean he's just some producer. We
talked about the role, and me maybe starring in another
movie that he wants to produce. I swear, that's it, Sean."
Sean exploded even more, "He wants to put the move on
my fucking family?" At the top of his lungs "My fucking
family!" He flipped the table over, breaking it. It was a
heavy table, but Sean is stronger than he looks.

I pleaded with him, "Sean, please!" He yelled at me,
"What?!" I tried my best to calm him down, "He probably
didn't know. It didn't come up. You're publicly dating
someone else. So…" He screamed at me, and it somehow
seemed even more intense, "So, you didn't tell him back
off?!" "Sean, I didn't…"

And then out of nowhere, he hit me with a chair.
I don't remember anything after that, until I woke up in a
hospital room. My arm was in a cast, hanging from a sling.
My face hurt. My eyebrow was in immense pain, as was
my lip. As I came to, the first face I saw, was of the man
that put me here.

Sean asked with concern in his voice, "How are you
feeling?" I responded, "Stay away from me." "I'm sorry.
I don't know what came over me. I-I…" "Save it for the
lawyers. Stay away from me!" We were in a private
hospital room, and no one would hear me. I could scream
like my life depended on it, but it wouldn't matter. If I did

ring for assistance, I wouldn't get any. He kept going, "I was just so jealous. You know how I am. You have…" he took hold of my left arm. The one that was not slung up in a cast, "You have our beautiful son. Our family. It's just…" At that point I had enough. "The one you slut-ed out right before giving birth? Are you fucking shitting me? Stay away from me. Don't come near me, or my kids." He continued to plead, "I'm sorry. Baby I promise, I'll never put my hands on you again. I swear." I've heard this song one too many times. I spoke through gritted teeth, "If you come near me or my kids again, I'll calling the cops." A flash of anger returned, "You would use my kid to threaten me?" but then he caught himself. "I understand you're angry…" I glared at him as I cut him off, "I'm serious Sean." He spoke blandly, with no energy "And tell them what, that you had a car accident. They'll pity you, that you hit your head." He was going to make me look crazy. They were going to believe him. He was a Kingpin. "You're a fucking bastard."

Sean spent the next six months helping me heal and working his way back into my life. And into my bed. I was so damned stupid. And of course, I wasn't cast for either movie.

From what I understand,
the producer died of pneumonia.

# CHAPTER 18:
## SWEET GOODBYES

Sean kept his word, for the most part. Until he didn't. I ended up pregnant again. He wanted energy from that, too. That would be my last sex party. My body will never be ravaged by so many people again, especially while I'm pregnant. What if something happened to the twins? After that, I wanted out. But when I tried dating someone else, they would end up dead. From pneumonia.

I knew Sean was behind it. This was not a coincidence. He gets jealous of a guy, and they die of pneumonia. I could be next. If I am going to get out of this alive, I am going to have to do something to make him stay away from me. I had a plan, but it's dangerous.

Sean has a vault where he keeps video tapes of all his 'conquests'. I started sleeping with him, again. After he falls asleep (he was starting to drink heavily), I would get into the vault and get a couple of the tapes, take them home, make copies, and swap them for the next set of tapes a few days later. It took weeks to get them all copied, and he never knew that I had them. This was my way out!

Some of the tapes had things I would never have expected, the gay parties are one thing, but the young boys, like Usher, Little Bow Wow, and Justin Bieber?! I would have never known. My God! Is he grooming Quincy? This has to end.

I invited him over one day, to confront him and put an end to our on-again-off-again relationship. He had entered my home unannounced for the last time. He would no longer have the key after today.

I was in the kitchen. Kimora and I were sharing drinks. I was scared to face him alone. Sean entered smiling, "What's up, Kimmy. Hey 'Mora." I told Sean, "Sit down." Because of my tone he looked at me stunned and asked, "What's going on? What is this?" I responded with delight, "Me taking my life back. We're done." He answered, "Hold on, wait a minute." I was so excited that I wasn't hearing any of it. I shouted at him, "No! No more. This is fucking over!" He looked confused as he asked, "Where is all of this coming from?" With disgust I said,    "I got the footage, Sean." He looked even more confused as he inquired, "What are you talking about?" Kimora said with revulsion, "Usher too?!" Sean said, "Wait. What the fuck is going on?"

Sean stood aggressively, and Kimora responded, "Don't make me call the cops." Sean's anger was creeping in as he replied, "This is how it is?!" I simply nodded. "If anything happens to either one of us, it gets released." He seethed as he queried, "After all I've done for you?" I don't think I was ever so happy as when I said those words to him. "Get out!" Pissed, he started to leave, looking back with pure hatred. As he walked down the stairs, he turned around in a fury, and lunged at me. He knocked me down near the top of the stairs. I was hurt. Kimora screamed, "Stop!"

As he began to crouch over me, I kicked at him, hitting him in the kneecap, then his face. He went tumbling down the stairs.   He was too hurt to get up. I called the cops. Kimora left before they arrived. When he left, it was in an ambulance. I felt empowered. I felt safe.

The Sean Combs days had finally come to an end.

CHAPTER 19:
FINALE

Things were okay, for a while. I started dating
again. It was almost normal until I got serious with
someone. Then my boyfriend died, of pneumonia. I knew it
was Sean. Again. That's when I decided to write this book.

A few days ago, my home was burglarized.
Only laptops were stolen. I know it was that bastard, or his
goons. Of course, I had a copy in the cloud, that I was able
to easily download here onto this new computer.

As I continue to write now, I'll send this into the
cloud as well. I will send out copies via email, and my
Google Drive password will be attached, so the missing
chapters can be accessed. This book must get out! There are
so many more chapters to add. This outline is a great start.
I have to organize the rest of the chapters and add them in,
little-by-little.

I planned on spending today working on exactly
that, but I'm not feeling very well. Thank God the kids
aren't here this weekend, so I can rest. I called Kimora to
cancel our tentative plans for a meetup. When I spoke to
her, she said, "Girl, that doesn't sound like the flu.
You want to go to the hospital?" That didn't immediately
alarm me. "I just need some rest.", I told her, and quickly
got off the phone.

But why can't I get my doctor? Why won't he pick
up the phone? Oh, no! I called Sean from my bedroom,
where I'm lying in my bed. All I could think about was the

kids. My babies who are with this monster. The man that I now suspect of having done this to me.

Sean picked up, with an air of superiority in his tone that let me know it was too late for me. He spoke confidently into the phone, "Hello." I screamed at him, "You bastard! I have your fucking children!" "What are you talking about? The kids are with me.", he replied with a mocking innocence. There's literally nothing I can do. I could only ask, "Did you ever love me?" Instead of answering the question, he responded, "The most important thing to me in the world, is loyalty." I couldn't believe it. I had to ask even though I understood, "What the fuck does that mean?" With the same feigned innocence, he mocked, "Kim, is something wrong?"

He's going to continue this game to the bitter end. I asked one last time, "How could you?" Again, with the narcissism I had now come to despise, he responded, "How could I? Do what? I gave you everything. You went to someone else. You left me just like everyone else did. You ask how could I? How could I what?" I yelled, "Look what you did to everyone around you!" There was only anger in his response, "So you're saying everyone leaves, because of how I am, and you were going to expose me?" He had me burglarized. I knew it. I shouldn't have threatened him, I should have just published the book.

I'm going to die, like Heavy D, like Biggie, like Pac, like so many others, and it's because he is a monster, plain and simple.

Before hanging up, I simply say, "That's not the only copy, you fuck!", then I shoot out a group tex t. I let everyone know, "He got me." Then I call 911.

As I sit here waiting for the ambulance, I am writing this chapter, and praying that I make it to the hospital. I don't feel like writing anymore. I may not be around to see it in print. It's okay. I'm sending it out. He won't get away with this!

I will have my say, my final words.
Sean Combs will get exposed,
even if I lose my life doing it.

My kids have always been my most cherished possessions.

I want the world to know that.

But more importantly,
I want them to know…

Made in the USA
Columbia, SC
22 September 2024

42802135R00033